Broken Record

Dallas Johnston

BookLeaf
Publishing

India | USA | UK

Presentation by *BookLeaf Publishing*

Web: www.bookleafpub.com

E-mail: info@bookleafpub.com

ISBN: 9789363316515

First edition 2024

To my daughters. Never doubt that you can do anything you set your mind to.

ACKNOWLEDGEMENT

To the people who have told me to put myself out there.
To the people who let me read drafts to them.
To the people who let me sit in silence and write.
To the people who don't understand poetry, but know that I am a poet.
To the people who never question my passions.

To my family, old and new.
To the students who allowed me to journey
with them.
To the writers, musicians, artists, and creatives who have helped me heal.

This one is for you.

PREFACE

This collection is many years in the making. Some of the poems have existed in tattered notebooks for years. Some have come to life in the notes app of a cell phone. Some were scrawled haphazardly during a work meeting or in the passenger's seat of the car. Whatever their origin, they speak to the complex existence that we all have to reckon with. These are words that have been brought to life because of moments, because of joy, because of pain. All the spinning emotions and experiences that we call life have inspired the hundreds of poems that it took to put together this collection. There are fifty-eight in this book, but there are so many more waiting to be presented to the world. I hope that reading them encourages you to funnel your own life experiences into your own type of art.

"I Carry Your Heart With Me"

Because lying in the darkness
to hide my silenced tears isn't enough
to purge the thought of you—

Because asking questions
that will remain unanswered
won't turn back the hands
of the biological clock—

Because one-tenth of your blood
runs through my orphaned veins.

Because like it or not,
I remember only the "good times"
and dancing in my own obliviousness—

Because even when the DNA
points like a broken compass to
a muddy stream of bad decisions—

I'm yours.

Because I carry your smile and
your crooked nose on my face,
your shame and your humor in my soul—

Because I wear plausible deniability
as rose-colored glasses
year after year after year—

Because I held your hand
as you shook off this mortal coil—
I carry your heart with me.

"Your Name"

Blustered breath held tight
within an ice-like fragile chest.

Thin-skinned palms damp
with anticipatory grief.

Syncopated
heartbeat.

And then I heard your name...

"How to Live in an Imaginary City"

How do we dance to deafening silence?
It becomes a movement controlled by
organic rhythms,
those produced within the soul.

How do we claim space in the absence
of millions?
We throw our arms out wide and inhale
the openness
of the concrete and the sand.

How do we stand tall when the weight of the
world is pressing against us?
By adding together the weight of
our collective spirits and pushing back.

How do we recover when all the bits of silver
and gold turn to paper and ash?
We start counting kindness and care as
the currency
of the moment and count ourselves rich.

"Paved Memories of the Time Before" (the night the lights went out in Vegas)

No obstructive uses.
Do not block the sidewalks.
Keep moving, keep moving.

Rubbing shoulders mile after mile.
Ducking into mirages to escape the heat.
Floating in a sea of strangers, all searching.

Searching for a jackpot, a yard of refreshment,
a glimpse at a white tiger,
1000 thread count sheets.

Everything that happens here, stays here.

But when what happens everywhere comes here
and stays here and subsequently sucks the
lifeblood from the city of lights…

It hurts.

It creates an obstruction to our way of life.
Our city that never dims becomes tired,
wounded, and slowly curls up and sleeps.

"Risen"

Third day phenomenon,
treacherous trails, tormenting trials

Questionable quest
to soul-deep resurrection

Another mountain to climb
while clamoring for earthly calm

When the hand of a familiar stranger
fills the cavern where hope used to be

Passing through the unknown in order
to maybe, someday, see the light again

Paradise promised if only the right
path emerges to the blind eye

Scaling an icy wilderness, desperate
to see a vulnerable splinter in the armor

Enduring the darkness of a racing mind
and a confused heart

Self-actualizing while compartmentalizing
the collective trauma of lost love

Risen from siloed despair by
the unexpected realization of maybe

A crack in the facade, a passage
to a new tomorrow.

"Bruises"

We all wanna
be somebody

Leave a mark,
be remembered

Be a bone-deep cut,
not a minor flesh wound

Yet, it's near impossible to
shine like a star

In a galaxy that comes at you
with high beams blaring

Just so it can drown out
your light.

"Healing"

Wounded by the weight of
the prickly and fickle world,
dizzy with decisions
about fate,
about future,
about futility,
a thousand tiny cuts
to the ego,
to the body,
to the soul.

Learning to unlearn the pattern
of swallowing the poisons of
the world,
the masses,
the judges,
the allies, and the foes.

Cleansing the psyche to emerge
new, whole, unfettered,
to be self-accepting,
to be self-actualizing,
to be autonomous,
so to be a cleaner slate.

Transforming the daily grind
into a mosaic of experience,
focusing on:
shouldering the weight,
lifting the spirit,
embracing the ambiguous,
realizing the possibilities,
to digest the richness of life.

Laying my broken wings
across the desert sand
with the intention of
transformation, transcendence,
fortitude, ferocity,
acceptance.

Letting the sunlight,
the moonlight,
the starlight,
cast shades
of doubtless gray
upon my sullied skin,

allowing it to absorb
the essentials of this life,
and the life yet to come.

Slowly, letting my
wounds become
the artifacts
of my survival,
so I can emerge
truer—
stronger—
emboldened—

Healed.

"The Lady Doth Protest Too Much"

It's like the knots in my back
will not let me think about the
things I should not do

The stress, the overwhelming
tidal wave of emotion being
suppressed by muscle memory

My agitated, thin skin tight yet
mind fragile not like petals,
but like trigger wires

The weight of the world
waiting to be lifted off my
sinking, sore shoulders

On repeat: another dime another
dollar, paid for with my time
and pieces of my common sense

Blinking just to sleep, sleeping
just to dream of a better
future—peace of mind

Tomorrow, a chance to
recount and reset, yet not
revisit the untidy ramifications

Photographic memory of
progress, progressing with
every declaration—pen to
paper process preeminent

Weeks like water, waves of
inspiration dripping through
fractured feelings—tears
fighting to be set free

Eye on the prize, heart
hardened so it will not break,
voice quaking, faltering but
secured in a cage of survival

Think it, don't say it, think
before you speak—speak up
for the voiceless, lower your
voice, don't speak unless spoken to

Measuring my moments—my
outcomes—my waist, but not
wasting my moments or
minimizing my momentum

Aching to see, to think, to feel,
to know that the ache in
my back means purpose

Shoulders steady—spine
braced, bones ready to bear
the burdens and the bounties

To lose the battle but
win the war with myself,
with the echo chamber,
with enemies real and perceived

To ultimately live the way
I was meant to live—
with purposeful pain,
with incalculable intensity.

"The Spice of Life: Black Cardamom"

Born in fire–
Hard to replicate–
Wrapped in black leather–
Vinyl records played too loud–
Rich with flavor–
An acquired taste–
Underlying profile of significance–
Controlled cardiac rhythm–
Kindling passion–
Distinct and intoxicating–
Burned by mental clarity–
Commanding, compelling–
Warm with a hint of sweetness–
Blends well with others–
Yet meant to stand out–
To be savored–
Magical and empowered–
Rough exterior, bitter center–
Essential–

A little goes a long way.

"Crushing It"

Rolling backward gracefully,
like a swan on roller skates

Ankles flexing, legs bending,
rolling like a water drop
on a stained glass window

Nothing but styled
choreography and
impressive moves

Gliding around and around
and around, at least in my
imagined version of this night

In reality, I am thirteen–
I am introverted–.
I am lonely–

There I sit, awkwardly
in a dark corner, pulling
at the orange laces of
my rented skates

Wishing to grab the loops of
his Calvin's and let him
guide me in a varnished
circle, into the night,
through my adolescence

Strobe lights, nacho cheese,
Lysol, and endless possibility

Hoping to one day
couple's skate while
New Edition serenades
a romanticized romance

In truth, I rarely left that corner,
never worked up the nerve

Just sat or circled the
boy in the faded black
jeans and neon skates

Friday nights at the
roller rink, where
imagined first loves
go to exist in limbo.

"Daydreams"

Foggy headed,
ignoring the
remains of the day

Space cadet extraordinaire,
lacking meaning, yet
always searching

Inhaling the clouds,
visions of excellence,
delusions of grandeur

A soul searching for
a safe place to wander

Every step another
way to become lost

Contemplating the
next moment,
the next path

Moments of clarity
interspersed with
a reality of confusion

Waking dreams giving
way to sleep paralysis

Seeing the invisible,
making it take shape
in the reality of the
day to day to day.

"Misunderstanding"

When words
get lobbed
like grenades

When actions scream

Intentional mishandling
of fragile feelings

Pouring more
emotional fuel
on the roaring
gaslighting

When the hits get
real and raw
and ugly

He calls it
a misunderstanding.

"Sorry Wrong Person"

A simple declaration,
a moment of vulnerable truth.

All thumbs, sharing thoughts
that could be dangerous.

Forgive me if I appear uncouth–
Why do I have this temporary
courage when I hide behind
six inches of metal and glass?

I am somehow stronger.

No fear of your response breaking
my heart and crushing my pride.

So I compose the lines,
fully compose myself–
full of determination to be heard,
to be real, to be seen...finally.

This will be the time you
embrace my truth, my imagination.

Who we are and who we can be
when the guises are dropped
fuels my need to be raw and confident.

To unleash my susceptibility to
the contagions of the midnight air.

This is it, I can't be stopped.

"Hi." You respond.
"Hey." "Can we talk?"
"Sure", you say.
"I need you", I begin,
allowing the levees to crack
and the unvarnished truth to flow.

"Don't leave like this–
Give us a chance to begin again.
I love you."

Three dots appear and disappear.
My heart stalls in my chest.
As they waiver between existing and not,
I anticipate your willingness.

Maybe this will be the one.
The time we finally hit close to the vest.

You respond, "Sorry, wrong person."

I become relegated to a texting pest.

"Fight Card"

The heart versus the head
an epic showdown between
rationality and emotion.

This would sell some tickets.
Whose side to be on?
The nation would be torn.
Families would suffer civil unrest.

On the night of the melee,
the heart would be draped in
glittery shades of red and pink,
assisted to the ring by a
fat, winged baby.

The head would enter boldly,
perched atop a pile of superfluous
bones and muscle and skin.

Flowing in on its own stream
of consciousness, dancing in
to its own iamb, the heart would
emote and sweat and cry a little,
giving no thought to the audience
or the atmosphere.

Critically aware and bordering on
hypersensitive, the head would
analyze and contemplate and
second-guess everything.

They would stare at one another,
sizing up the competition.

The heart would think he was in love,
the head would see the heart as
weak and fallible.

With a Laaaaddddiiieeesss and geeeentlemeeeen,
in this corner...

The announcer would set the battle in motion.

Millions of spectators would rise to their feet,
both ringside and in living rooms.
Expecting visible carnage of oxygenated
blood and brain matter.

Vicarious fans dressed in overpriced
t-shirts in support of their imagined victor.
Waiting with bated breath either scrutinizing
or internalizing every move.

The heart would strike first, bowling
the head over with vulnerability,
leaving him disoriented, grappling
for facts, but he'd retaliate with
word problems and logic.

Heart and head would see the other
as a formidable adversary.

After ten rounds, the contenders
dragged to their corners, they'd
lock eyes from across the ring.

At the next bell, they'd stagger,
punch-drunk, to the center,
embrace each other until the
bout is called a draw.

The crowd simultaneously
mouthing REMATCH.

No arms raised in victory,
a crowd feeling hollow and cheated.

No purse collected, no
comically large belt awarded.

Nothing but empty cups and broken dreams.

Rematch being inevitable, as this conflict
is perpetual, morning headlines ready in
all capital letters:

HEART AND HEAD HAVE UNFINISHED
BUSINESS.

"Mirror"

28

Lie to me
and tell me
I'm just a
pretty face

Let me wander
through you
into a world
I can call
my own

Remain unbroken
until I am ready
to slit my
fantasies wide open

Show me the
backwards past
that is right here
yet untouchable

Make left become
right as reality
warps into fiction

Let me be a glass
mannequin gazing
blankly into
mere heated sand

Lie to me and
tell me
I am just
your reflection.

"Take These Tears"

Stir your morning coffee
with a salted spoon

Prepare your watery memories
to face another day

Breathe your words deep
into your briny lungs,
hidden from declaration

Walk with salient silence into
the dusk of another day

Wash away the saline, take
these tears, pour them
into an indeterminable tomorrow.

"Encircle Me in Yellow"

31

Slice the fruit of the earth
and fold me inside of it

A molded embrace of
replicated sunshine

The Alpha and Omega
of golden hope

Soured sweetness peppered
by amber petals and buttered skies

Encircle me in yellow
so I can taste it on
my tongue and feel
its blonde warmth
travel through
my lemon veins.

"If I Could"

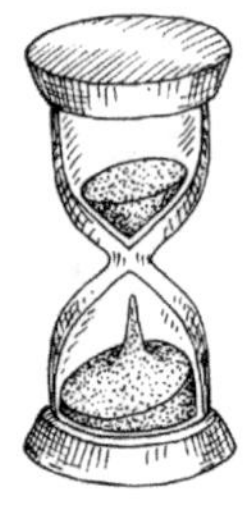

I'd hand-pluck each grain
of sand
from the hourglass
of my life

I'd run counterclockwise
in an effort to undo
the misstepped moments

I'd speak in a
riddled, backwards jargon
to unsay
my last words
to you.

"The Song I Wrote For You"

Not quite a love song
more like a ballad
of passive-aggressive
passion

A kind of metal overture
of emotional heart
rhythms and
melodious outcries

An amalgamation
of bass and drums
and remorse

A way to tell the
stories of a complicated,
complex, and
confusing life

Sick with syncopation,
heavy with the need
to stay radio-friendly while
not selling out

The not-so-subliminal
messages etched into
every groove

The perfect one-hit
wonder, wondering if
you'll take the time
to listen to the
entire song.

"The Sound of Water"

35

Serpentine, breathing
through invisible gills

Flowing with the flow,
tapping resolutely against
glass and stone

Inhaling the rush of
tides and waves

Like birth—
like rebirth—
like catharsis—

Lending its melody
to the orchestra
of the air and the sky

The sound of water
mirrors life at its
tumultuous best.

"Beguiled"

Today is the day
I say goodbye to
the papier-mâché
proselytizers

The day that I
realize that a halo
doesn't always make
you holy, only
holier than thou

The day that I bid
farewell to self-righteousness
and begin the journey
into the valley of the shadows

Today is mine—

The gates have burst
open, a chance to be
welcomed into whatever
level I choose to exist in

Cleansed in
fire–
water–
earth–
or air–

Walking an illuminated
path toward one
of many judgments

Seeking guidance from
no one or everyone,
my own choice,
my own free will

Choosing to swim across
a boiling lake or encapsulate
myself in a prison of ice

My choosing, today is mine—

No more social media
sermons delivered
by hollow men
who deem
themselves hallowed

Today I see that slight
of hand conceals more
than what meets the eye

Today I let no beast mislead
me, no guardian misdirect me,
no companion misadvise me

Today I learn to be the
conductor of my own
spiritual resurrection.

"With Ease"

It is easy to fade into
an invisible disaster

Learning to cry in the darkness, mastering
the ability to smile through pain,
trudging on, even when
the world becomes quicksand

Embracing a mediocre existence like you
were born to be subpar and live
to be underwhelming

Blending into the vanilla sunset of each
passing day, knowing that tomorrow will
be yet another disappointment

Flying beneath love's radar while
limboing under your own
low standards

It is inevitable to fade into
an invisible disaster.

"Signs of Life: Las Vegas"

(When a global pandemic falls upon a city that never sleeps)

Don't go breaking my heart,
it may look like metal, but it is merely glass.
This is a city of illusion.
You know that's not the actual
Eiffel Tower, right?

Approximately 4.2 miles of plaster paradise,
built on escapism, fantasy, silver, and paper.
Sky-high structures that offer a trip around the
world in a weekend
if you walk fast enough.

Overnight, the lights began to dim.
Paris, Egypt, New York City, all reduced to
abandoned pieces of architecture.
No bells, no whistles, no midnight
steak and eggs.

Who would have thought that all you had to do
to wash away the sins of a city was
lock the doors, shut off the lights,
and wait for its heart to stop beating.

"In Case of Emergency"

Prepare to siphon fuel
from the soul of the collective

Pack a go-bag: fill it with
resilience, self-reliance

Break glass ceilings,
take the elevator to floor 13

Refuse the status quo,
innovate without fear

Bend with the storm,
but refuse to break

Burrow deep inside yourself,
bracing for emotional impact

Stockpile love and tenacity,
prepare to withstand emotional torrents

Find solace in the silence,
surrounded by the hope of survival

It is possible, to endure the
things that threaten to destroy us

In case of emergency, know you
have the tools to save yourself.

42

"In a Long Time"

43

We won't wonder when wonder withered.
Sudden stillness secured simply, steadily.

Letting laughter languish, lull,
listlessly lingering.
Nature necessitating nonchalant numbness.

Happenstance happening haphazardly,
forgetting functional folly, forgiving foolishness.

Guiding gratuitous grief graciously.
Beholding beauty before bedlam.

Turning timepieces tenuously.
Thinking that time transcends trials,
tearing through twilights, testing tranquility.

Gathering generosity, grace, and gratitude.
Grand gestures, glorious glimpses.
Reverent recklessness, riotess rewards.

"Walls that Are No Longer Home"

Deafening darkness where
there used to be loud light

Hollow happiness bouncing
between plaster and wood

Echos wrestling with shadows,
memories fighting for survival

Breathless body of endless
hallways and terminal life.

"Navy Blue Loss"

(Dedicated to a life gone too soon)

No one thinks that today will be their last day.
Waking in the morning, the taste of sleep
in their mouth,
a slight crease pressed into their skin
from the texture of cotton sheets,
after surrendering into dreamless sleep.

Brain churning awake, accepting this new day,
heart pumping today's blood into today's veins,
body ready to labor through today's
uphill climb.

It's senseless to have to mourn you right now.

Sunup to sundown, switching from raw
humanity to automated, socially acceptable self,
diligently running on the wheel of an
undervalued life.

No one thinking that today another gun
will take another life,
that someone's journey will cease
in year nineteen,
right when it should have been starting.

It's senseless to have to mourn you right now.

With prom dresses and university t-shirts
adorning your recent photos, no one thought
that they would rise on this day to learn
that your image would be frozen in youth.

I can't imagine the pain and the
weight of the grief
that sits upon your loved ones,
the heaviness they
now must bear, hearts feeling pecked,
as if ravenous birds of loss exist to
remind us all
that this is the world we live in.

It's senseless to have to mourn you right now.

Mornings in America are now for mourning
the loss of another mother, another child,
another member of this or that community.

This navy blue loss weighs on my heart
as I grapple with mixed emotions:
the fear, the sadness, the anger, the regret.

We have learned to walk through our days
as so many hollowed-out shells, restricted
from emotion, reaction, or opinion.

It's senseless to have to mourn you right now.

Is this the world we are willing to accept?
Advocacy isn't a mouse click away, it is time
to make demands. Demand that our neighbor,
our daughter, our friend, isn't the next to die.

Time to disrupt the comfort of
covering hard truths
with a blurry, socially-safe
haze of indifference.

We can't let this become another
navy blue loss
decorated with sentiment
but not addressed by action.

It's senseless to have to mourn you right now.

"Moonlight"

If stillness
whispers to it…

If man can transform
beneath its stream…

If romance equates
to walks in it…

If it can light
the darkest of nights…

I, too, am moonlight.

"If You Forget Me"

If you forget me, do it quickly, so I
can disappear without
a trace

Scrub me from your amnestic
being, and gift me back
my wings

Forge forward leaving my
divergent path
yet untread

Disremember the history,
distance our stories, our
bodies, and our souls

Forget me, abandon fidelity,
exonerate my heart from duty,
free it from its gilded cage

If you forget me, let me forget
you, without the burden
of granting forgiveness.

"Goodbye & Hello"

A midnight stumble down
a darkened street

Me, draped in the arms of a rebound,
cuddled in regret

Our eyes locking,
if only for a brief moment

Flashing back to the reasons
we never deserved each other.

"Broken Pen"

No words, no will.
Detachment, sadness,
broken tomorrows.

Indifference, confusion,
misguided inky rage.

Numbed regret provoked
by sorted silence.

Arid tear ducts, bloodless veins,
wordless war cries lasting days.

Invisible conversation,
scribbled by a broken pen.

"In the Moment"

You met me at a very strange time in my life.

Doubt flowing through me like vinegar,
confusion coursing through
every part of me.

Sleepless nights and restless days,
all adding up to weeks and months of mixed
metaphors falling on deaf ears.

Passion project or purposeful purpose?
When is it not strange to accept
naivety and embrace
change, evolution, and unlearning?

Inconvenient truths are conveniently ignored,
blind hearts multiplying like spores, blocking
the view of what is real.

It will take work, it will take discomfort.
We must be ready to face the arena,
throw down our shields
and refuse to tangle for the
enjoyment of the masses.

That vinegar will transform into a sweet wine.
That confusion into a healthy curiosity.
That language, once foreign, will
roll from the tongue.

You met me at a very strange time in my life.

But when will it be a better time? Never.
The time is now, it has always been now,
we were just not ready to shoulder the burden.

"Garden of Glass"

54

Germination of determination.

Blooms of banality,
seeds of shame.

Self-sown conditionality,
transplanted organic will.

Perennial life expectancy,
scarification by intimidation.

Indeterminate heart planted,
as heirloom stalks sway.

Companion planting grains
of patience, willing them to thrive.

A hopeful bringer of life
with an unfortunate black thumb.

Wishing to be a marigold
in a forest of walnut trees.

"Honey Dipped Tulips"

55

When the intonation
of your uncertain
voice triggers doubt

When a subtle
gesture screams like
the tremors will
soon become earthquakes

When the vase finally cracks
and the pressure of watery words
starts as a slow leak,
and manifests into a flood

When sunlight and subtlety no longer
nurture delicate petals,
and sweetness cannot remedy
imminent death

When simple, organic love
will no longer flow through the iridescence,
the honey-tongued presence
of your false promises finally fail.

"20/20 Vision"

We used to think space
was the great unknown.
Science the savior,
keeping harm at bay.

Then it came.
The fear.
The uncertainty.
The loss.
The unfamiliar.

Warm faces and wide smiles
reduced to inch-high squares
and paper mysteries.

Mics on, unmuted reality,
months of transformation
and zoomed in communities.

Inventiveness the height
of survival, surviving the
monotony of another sunrise.

Longing for the normalcy of
a day where shaking hands
and kissing babies is okay.

Day and night blurred by
the inopportune arrival of
a phantom menace.

We used to think that we
were invulnerable to attack,
until overnight we became victims.

Then it came.
Then we endured.
Then we healed.
Then we changed.
Then we survived.

20/20 vision in the rearview.

"First Flush of Love"

Remember the feeling?
The one that starts in the belly and
rushes through the heart and mind?

The way it feels to choke down a breath
and hold it in while you swallow meaning.
The way it feels to know that you have
encountered something that will change
the way you see and explain the world.

Digesting every syllable, letting it
nourish every part of you.
Finding a place to house it,
inviting it to live in you
'til death do you part.

Remember the feeling?
Of understanding, for the first time
the incredible power and purpose
of words? The palpable realization
that every emotion can be encased
in a mere jumble of letters.

That somewhat arbitrary rule that this
combination means love, that one hate.
Two letters can eviscerate and
twelve can congratulate.

Never underestimate the absolute power of
words: written, whispered, released, or
held captive, they are powerful nonetheless.

Like nothing else in the real or imagined world,
they can be harnessed as a weapon of mass
creation or one of mass destruction.

I remember when I first fell in love. I remember
the last time I fell in love. I fall in love almost
every day with a new word or phrase.

"Blue, uncertain, stumbling buzz."
"Let us go then you and I."
"Abandon all hope ye who enter here."
"To be great is to be misunderstood."

These are the love letters of my
benign life, the alphabet soup
that keeps my passion burning and my
blood pumping, so I can produce more words.

I try to always remember the feeling of
purchasing vulnerabilities
through the currency
of letters, words, and phrases in order
to buy passage into the uncharted
territory of the next phase of my life.

Holding deep in my soul's memory,
that first flush of love that urged me
to never forget that my true love
is inky and leaden and found buried
inside the imagination and talents
of so many who have come before me.

"The Invisible Life of a Fictional Prince"

I am a man and I am a son.
The duty of a man is to exhibit
strength and to rule his emotions or
his home or even his kingdom—
The duty of a son is to appease
and hopefully please his father.

My call of duty is not that of most men,
maybe because I am not like most men—
I am intellectual, poetic, romantic,
and this is my internal burden—
"Avenge me," speaks my father's ghost,
make me proud, be an honorable man.

My hands know nothing of doubling into fists,
they prefer a delicate grip on a quill—
Fashioning wit into words that will win a heart
or bury a foe in a pun; I am no fighter—
Yes, I can wield a sword, my father
paid the best coaches to ensure it.

Now the time has come to slay the beast that
stole my father's life and his wife, my mother—
I am a man and I am a son and it is my duty
to abide by the wishes of the king, my father—
Even in death he challenges my artistic side
forcing it to burrow deep and
hide from the world.

"Avenge me," I am told, and my world
turns upside down in an instant—
I wander the majestic castle sabotaging
my mind,
my love life, and the relationship with my
mother—
Even if I live, murdering will kill my soul,
I am no fighter; I am afraid.

Paralyzed, I can only evoke self-doubt which
escapes in the form of questions and
soliloquies—
"To be or not to be" plagues my mind as I
attempt to be a good son
and an honorable man—
Death intrigues me, as it is the most
final answer to the suffocating
question of life.

Father, I have tried to be your son, your prince,
and your hero, but I am flawed and confused—
My life has been one of privilege and
circumstance, I followed your rules but you
forgot one thing—
A man can be measured in more ways than one,
father, he can be measured by
his ability to love.

All I wanted was to be your prince,
your son, your savior,
but not the one you groomed me to be—
I wanted to be your son, the one with the wife,
the children, and the approval of his father—
Unfortunately, the blood in my veins and the
love in my heart was not enough to please you.

I'm sorry, my father, my king.
I am not the son you wished for—
I am Prince Hamlet of Denmark,
a mess of a man drowning in
an existential crisis—
Trying with all his might to avenge you
in a blaze of glory like you deserve.

All you will get from me, father, are
words, want, and the will to appease you—
But that will never be enough to avenge your

good name, I will stumble and fail
and self-critique—
Eventually, my want to be the man
you wished for
will lead me to hurt all those I love.

I am a man and I am a son,
and I will die feeling like
I failed at being both.

"Emily Dickinson"

What is it about a woman with
a pen that scares people?

She was one of many who
quietly mastered how to
build a metered and measured
dam to hold back just the right
amount of what could be
a destructive force.

She knew, like the white-clad profit
that she was, that her every move would
be scrutinized, analyzed, weaponized.
That her mere femininity would disqualify
her from the race of creative life.

She, like a scientist, a wordologist,
assembled without instruction, a world
of words and confessions, using only
a single, rudimentary tool.

With the precision of an architect,
she drafted a life story of a woman
who broke rules, who defied
expectation, who loved dangerously
and knew that her vulnerabilities
would be cross-examined by an ever-judgmental
and unaccepting world—both present and future.

Because some things never change,
her womanness was subjected to
microscopic examination—
her white dress not a thick enough skin
to protect her from the watchful eye
of the status quo.
Alone and maybe lonely, she married
words to paper with a harmony that
did not exist in her own world.
Raising questions of her own will
for mortality and the methods
behind her supposed madness.

Slanting to get the right view of
the world she wished to live in,
a seminarian soul in the body
of a creative, she planted
herself in a garden of her
own creation.

Nothing but a window-sized
view of the world, she saw life,
death, and love through the
telescope of her pen.

Feeling deeply isn't reserved for
those with unconditional wanderlust.
For jailing the body doesn't also
jail the mind.

Emily, if I may call her Emily,
found her voice on loose scraps
of stationary, which existed in
their own private context, until
they made their way to a
leather-bound reality.

Everything from her syncopation to her
secrets have found a place to call home
somewhere in the recesses of minds,
hearts, passions, tattoos.

An accidental icon who was brushed off
as a broken woman who couldn't write
poetry. A woman whose value of love
was determined to be zero, a woman
who armed with a pen, drew a map
for how to live without apologies.

"Power Suit"

Tailored to fit the mold we are placed in
by the rules and regulations of what it
means to be powerful

Structured shoulders stitched to
bear the weight of the world,
to square the body in preparation to
meet the demands of the arbitrary masses

Defined by thread color, like roses with
varied meanings, each hue sending a
subliminal message

A perfectly sewn metaphor for
what it means to have touched the
pinnacle of success

Like the duality of a superhero
the suit transforms perception:
ordinary to extraordinary

What magnificent deeds will the suit
call for? What accomplishments will
it support that could never be
done in simple denim?

How will it puppeteer the greatness that
only a suit will allow? How will it enable the
wearer to assert a place in the
social hierarchy?

Powerful perfection, perfectly creased.

Faith that the threads will serve
as anchor stitches, continually weaving
together the flesh and the fabric

Little did they know, that the power of the
power suit was woven deep within the soul
of the wearer all along.

"Poem"

In a world that feels like
it is made of sand,
it feels impossible to build
a safe space
for difficult truths

When the simplest action
is as dangerous
as disarming a bomb

When you work to make
yourself bulletproof—
finding out that the ammo
is armor piercing—
leaving emotional
shrapnel that never
disappears and never heals

We withdraw—
We isolate—
We detach—

We become grains
of sand lacking
the fortitude to withstand
the bluster and betrayal
of even the most
innocuous breeze

Slipping through the years
like they were a sieve,
scrambling to secure
our footing only to
backslide into uncertainty.

"Let Them Eat Cake"

Even in a castle, there are skeletons in the closet,
rattling in the darkness behind
old coats and discarded memories

Marble floors and gold-gilded fixtures
do little to mask the shallow interior
of a fragmented past and
an uncertain future

Tossing crumbs to those who revel in
the thought of hovering near the
perimeter of the inner circle

The blue light glow that captures
the perfectly curated life scripted
in hashtags and filtered photos

Feeding an insatiable hunger without
ever feeling satisfied, only
craving attention never substance

Deep conversation never uttered,
never politics, nor religion, nor the
meaning of life, the talk stays small

The cyclical existence of supply
and demand perpetuated one
networking event at a time

Always a handshake but never a handout,
fiscal conservatism a fine term for
let them eat cake.

"The Quilt"

I live in a wooden shed in the backyard,
its basic wooden walls not shielding me
much from the desert sun

Hidden behind the fabricated edifice, I miss
the ladies who used to place me in the
center of the gossip circle

Even in here, I have outlived
the stories and the memories,
the flesh and the blood

I am a survivor, even if meant to
live out my existence
in a plastic bin next to rusted tools

Put away, but not forgotten,
ready to be called up for the duty
of evoking nostalgia

Knowing my stitches can heal
and mend, warm and comfort,
under even not-so-perfect circumstances

Aging but alive, bringing
hope and closure to open emotional
wounds or closed familial paths.

"The Perfect Mixtape"

The vibrato of teen angst
blending seamlessly with the
synthesized bass of hip-hop,
telling stories of youthful
idealism and heartbreak

That song you remember
from family road trips
and the one that takes
you back to a first kiss

A one-hit wonder by a band
you are embarrassed to love,
and an obscure b-side single

A musical journey through
decades and moments,
a joyride of genres with
no rhyme or reason

Lyrics that say everything
that was left unsaid,
musically illustrating
a unique life journey

Van Morrison.
The Smiths.
Otis Redding.
Concrete Blonde.
Sublime.
Elvis.
The Beastie Boys.
A Tribe Called Quest.
R.E.M.
Squeeze.
Panic at the Disco!
Joan Baez.
Joy Division.
Bad Religion.

All that and more,
a lifetime of drowning
in audio to celebrate,
to heal, to revel, to dance.

"Change Your Narrative"

78

One less yes
a few more no's

A day of stillness
to counteract too
many days of hustle

Blasting music to
muffle the sounds
of life

Allowing breath to
slow and flow

Unlike the strangling
lack of air that forces
its way into
our daily lungs

Choosing to trade
wine for water

To drive the open
road instead of
the information
superhighway

Self-sacrifice is
only sanctified if
the sacrifice is
truly selfless

Sacrificing the self
the mind, the body,
the soul

Will only lead
to an empty
vessel

One who
cannot be
re-poured into

Constantly subtracting
from, never adding to

Sacrifice for
the self;
do not
sacrifice the self.

"Signs of Intelligent Life"

You can scour the arid desert
far beyond the noise of the
burning light

You can stumble under the
shadowed skies searching
for the perfect sign

You can peek between the
moments, explore the silence
and the chaos

You can wander, wondering
if the universe is trying to
tell you something

You can listen to the echo
of subtle conversations, letting
them direct the search

You can collect clues, gathering
pieces of a cosmic puzzle that
exist on the outskirts of understanding

You can make eye contact
with a dozen strangers, hoping
to glimpse into at least one soul

You can sift through personalities
like a societal archeologist, unearthing
nuance and idiosyncrasy

You can continue to grasp at
straws, hoping to catch a trace
of meaning before it slips away

You can.
You can.
You can.

Nothing is haystacking the needle
of intelligent life but the refusal
to harness the impossible
strength of patience

Nothing is camouflaging
the social complexity of
endless possibility and
the hope of a better future.

"Resurrection"

82

Pry out the nails
that attach your
self-worth to
his opinions

Lower yourself
from the crossroad
of stay or go

Walk, even on
wounded feet,
toward a
new beginning

Journey for three
days, or weeks, or years,
until you choose
the sunrise that
will light
your resurrection

Born anew
proving that stigma
can be shed,
and scars of
emotional stigmata
can be worn
like badges
of survival

Rise and discard
the flesh of
that once broken
woman, and
inhabit the new
skin of freedom

Burn the bridge
that once led
you to pain

Dive head first
into the holy
waters of life,
and emerge
into a world
you can call
your own.

"Underestimated"

84

Look closely and
you'll see my—
delicacies

A pastel exterior,
presumably fragile

Look closer and
you'll see a body—
that can withstand
a violent storm

A natural armor
hidden beneath
my petals

Mistaken for a thing
of only external beauty

An unknown phenomenon
filled with more
power and strength–
than they will
ever understand.

"Womanhood"

Without words
I am left to wonder

Without signs
I am left to wander

Without reality
I am left with wishes

Without fruit
I am left to wither

Without hope
I am left to wrestle

Without acceptance
I am left to withdraw

Without empathy
I am left to weaken

Without equality
I am left to withstand

With my own wit
I will weather the
work that weaves
body with mind
with willpower

I am a woman—
Not wounded—
Not wingless—
Not wordless—

I am a woman.
Brandishing the
world's most
powerful weapons—
wonderment and
willingness

Wrecking
glass
floors,
walls,
and
ceilings.

"Vast Possibility"

I have been wearing
the ocean all day

The salt settling
on my skin

Sun-kissed and
brittle from the
briny embrace
of a miracle

Allowing myself
to be reborn of nothing
but foam and
waves and motion

Shedding the
ornaments of an
ordinary life and
embracing the ebb
and flow of living
by the power
of the moon

I've been wearing
the ocean all day
welcoming the slow
erosion of my
plastic shell

The sand and the
power and the calm
strength of the
elements turning
the tide of a yesterday
into a new tomorrow.

"Red Queen"

She doesn't want your
painted roses

She doesn't want power
or responsibilities

She puts on a tough
front but it's as
fake as the garden
she exists in

She doesn't want
the endless rabbit
hole of expectations

She doesn't want
the doublespeak
and the riddles

She hides the volume
of her own demands

She insulates herself
with nonsense
She doesn't want
this phony existence

She wants to let her
hair down and see the
wonderland through
reality tinted glasses

She just needs a quiet
garden blooming with
authenticity where she
can whisper her ideas

She wants to sit at the table
sipping the tea of friendship
and love and realness

She wants real blood to flow
when the thorns of life
prick her into realization

She wants imperfection
and pain and love and
no map but her own
intuition to guide her

She wants to drop the facade
and admit that she never
ever liked croquet.

"Stolen"

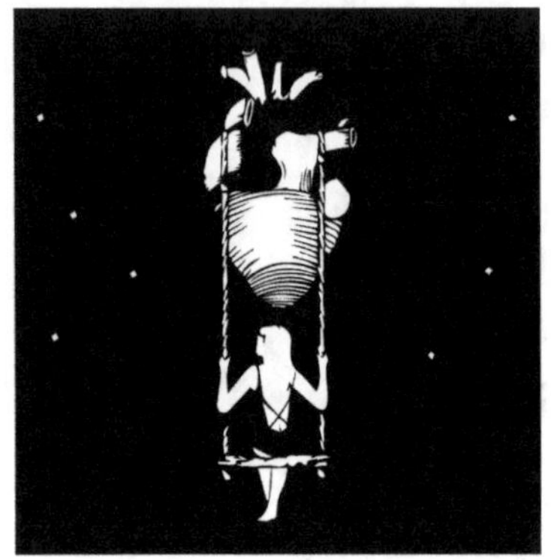

Youth.
Innocence.
Breath.
Heart.
Property.
Moments.

Taken, not returned.
No permission given.
True story.

"Regret"

93

The last
sip.

The last
word.

The last
glance.

The end.

"Duality"

94

Rise and shine,
time to prepare
today's face for
what we will
be asked to
face today.

Feeding the soul
with whatever it
takes to fill it
with gratitude.

Out the door
headstrong, headed
to the remains
of the day.

Like a masquerade,
two faces prepared
to face the faces
of the everyday.

"Bouquet"

As Prufrock was no Hamlet,
I am no Ophelia.
You will never find me
surrounded by flowers
handing out my madness.

I may wander down
deserted streets and
question my place in
the questionable world,
but I will never fall
hopelessly into
my own sorrow.

On those days when
drowning isn't even
a strong enough metaphor,
my resilience can be
used as a floatation device.

"Finally"

Standing in a hallway
defending myself from
your unsolicited advice,

I'll wrap my composure
tightly around me and
silently and steadfastly
deflect your unwanted
verbal advances.

In the end, you were
the first to leave.
I overcame the urge
to placate you, never
accepting your
invitation to dance.

Today I place a rose,
mostly thorns, on the
soil you sleep in.
Celebrating the fact
that I can stand
above you and no
longer behind you.

"Do I Dare"

Dedicated to T.S. Eliot

Disturbing the universe is a personal goal,
constantly battling imposter syndrome
for a chance to reach my potential

There will be time, there will be time,
to iterate and iterate and iterate myself,
my purpose, the answers to my questions

Decisions, revisions, and the sheer will
to see my greatness reach its pinnacle,
drives me through fight, flight, and freeze

Daring to break the mold I was cast in,
rolling up my sleeves to bracelet my
arms with bent coffee spoons

Measuring the meaning of each daily
action by empty cups, approving nods,
and untarnished accomplishments

The evenings, the mornings, the
afternoons, they have forgiven my
transgressions and celebrated my successes

When will I be able to celebrate myself?
Will it be after tea and cake and crisis?

"Sorry Not Sorry"

Excuse me while
I put my philosophy
away for your
personal comfort.

Allow me to compromise
my morals to satisfy
the status quo.

Watch me close
the door and open
minds without
your advice.

See me embrace judgment,
discomfort, and disappointment,
all for the greater good.

Remember me turning
the other cheek,
picking up my stride,
and carrying on.

"Beyond the Neon"

When I look out the window of
my suburban home
there are cars and dogs, and hedges for miles.
A vanilla neighborhood of fifty shades of beige,
homogenizing the inhabitors
of this tract dreamland.

Ironically, this innocuous neighborhood
exists right on the border
of the sinniest of cities.
A fabricated, neon fantasy built on
debauchery and hedonism,
urging what happens here to stay here.

For decades I have been sin approximate.
Growing up in the glow of light pollution,
lulled to sleep by the metallic clang
of coin on metal.
Breathing in the dry heat and soaking in the
desert sun, one hundred degrees at a time.

Inside the walls of our landscaped oasis
we are removed from the chaos that is
an ever-growing metropolis.

It is easy to separate the twenty-four
hour town from the day-to-day
demands of a somewhat normal life.

When others imagine a weekend in
our city, they see the opportunity
for escapism and forgetfulness.
Forgetting that in the heart of any
wonderland are the hatters and
queens, the players, and the watchers.

A 4.2 mile divide between normalcy
and neon, a sky high margin of
real life and fantasy.
Alarm clocks and coffee pots
arming the ordinary to tackle life
on the outskirts of other
people's wildest dreams.